~~est friends of my
life — Love you!!

Shelley

ONE STRAY SHEEP

EVERLEE RISING

WESTBOW
PRESS®

A DIVISION OF THOMAS NELSON
& ZONDERVAN

WestBow Press books may be ordered through booksellers or by contacting:

WestBow Press
A Division of Thomas Nelson & Zondervan
1663 Liberty Drive
Bloomington, IN 47403
www.westbowpress.com
1 (866) 928-1240

ISBN: 978-1-9736-7583-9 (sc)
ISBN: 978-1-9736-7582-2 (e)

Print information available on the last page.

WestBow Press rev. date: 10/11/2019

I want to dedicate this book to my son. I wrote this for you squirrel. I hope God speaks to your heart when you are old enough to read it. I also want to thank my aunt for always praying for me and believing in me.

CONTENTS

INTRODUCTION

I will start with His words and not mine. John 8:12 reads:

> When Jesus spoke again to the people, he said, am the
> light of the world. Whoever follows me will never walk
> in darkness, but will have the light of life."

I was saved as a kid and then spent most of my life straying. As a result, my soul yearned in sadness for God's presence. On top of that, my straying opened the door to the devil. He was able to enter my mind with no barrier and attack me. I was helpless to this attack and he almost destroyed me. Guess what? I am still here and not only did God save me from complete destruction but He is now using me for his glory. Why? When you are saved, you become a sheep in God's flock. If you stray outside of the flock and become lost, He does not stand by and watch you go. He follows you hoping to lead you back. I used to think of my life as one long drama filled with pain and disappointment. Now I realize that my life is a love story. I have walked through this life in rebellion and came out on the other side a survivor. I owe this to God. He has loved me all along. He watched me turn away from him and run and I now know this grieved Him. He followed me with a patience I cannot comprehend because He loves me. He loved me before I was born. Because of His love for me, He followed me. He followed me through my sin as I walked along the crevice of Hell blindfolded. By His grace, I felt his presence and turned back. The moment I did, He forgave me and restored me. Now I walk with God every day and His love resides in my heart. My existence has gone from lonely and painful to full of joy and peace. I want you to read this love story in hopes that you too will understand what God's love means for your future. The devil attacks those who stray after salvation and he uses many different weapons to destroy their lives. He will use words, lies, distractions, temptations and persuasion. Only when we return to our walk with God can we harness the power we have over the devil. And only then can we experience true victory in our lives. I want to share this with you so that you may know that it is never too late to turn back. Your sin is never too grave. His grace is sufficient. Do you believe you have been too bad for too long and now you don't deserve mercy or maybe now you fear turning to God? A repentant heart need not fear and God's arm is long enough to reach anyone. His mercy runs deeper than you can dig. And you would be right about not deserving His mercy. God's mercy is a gift. It cannot be earned. Romans 3:10-12 says:

> As it is written: There is no one righteous, not even one; there is no one who understands, no one who seeks God. All have turned away; they have together become worthless; there is no one who does good, not even one.

The Bible then goes on to explain that Jesus died for our sins bringing salvation and righteousness to those who believe. Even while we were still sinners, Jesus died to save us.

Romans 5:5 says:

> And hope does not disappoint us, because God has poured out his love into our hearts by the Holy Spirit, whom he has given us.

Remember that even though you have been saved, you will never be perfect here on Earth. We are to walk with God obeying his commands and loving others. If you stray, it doesn't mean that God stops loving you. God's love is unconditional and never ends. We are the ones who own ever changing hearts. We are the ones who turn from God and not the other way around. If we repent with a contrite heart, He is quick to forgive. Then we can return to the flock and walk in the light of His guidance.

LOVE STORY

LOVE STORY

God has been chasing me my whole life. I have been running from Him my whole life, until now. I finally figured it out. I turned to God and now I have unspeakable peace and joy. My insides are calm, my heart is glad, and my cup literally overflows. This comes from a woman who spent most of her adult life broken, depressed and apathetic. I have wandered through this life desperate to know why my life seemingly held no meaning or purpose. The pain I lived with on a daily basis can only be explained by saying that I lived in my own personal prison of madness. I have been depressed most of my life. It never made logical sense to me. I had a great childhood and I had some wonderful people in my life growing up. I spent years meditating on it and trying to figure it out. Was I sexually abused and if so, would that experience color my spirit forever? The fact is, I am not sure if I was or not. I have a memory of something that happened to me when I was around seven years old that has floated in and out of my mind my whole adult life. A neighbor told me to get into his truck one day. I can remember the exact conversation we had. I can also remember the make and color of his truck. I remember getting into the truck and then nothing and I remember getting out. That is it. Part of my sadness in life has always been that I didn't understand its source. Why did I always feel so full of pain? Was it because my parents divorced? Was it because I had a chemical imbalance? Was I just crazy? Well, the factors involved in my life experience are actually not important. No one goes through life without tragedy. What was important, is important is the status of our relationship with God. If you have been saved at some point in your life, you have been born again. In other words, if you have received Jesus as your Lord and Savior then you are no longer your own. You are purchased by the blood of Jesus and you have become one of His children, chosen for an eternity spent in Heaven with God. John 3:16 says:

> For God so loved the world that he gave his only begotten son, that whoever believes in him shall not perish but have everlasting life.

Think about this for a minute. God, the creator, the sovereign Lord over everything, the ruler of the universe, the king of all kingdoms, the beginning and the end has made a way for us to be reconciled to Him. He loves us, sinners, so much that He sent His son Jesus to die on a cross as a substitute for our sin. Jesus was born of a virgin, walked a life of perfect righteousness, died on a cross for our sins, and rose three days later from the grave. He ascended to Heaven where He sits on a throne at the right hand of the Father. This was done out of love as a gift and whoever believes it, will be saved. We are saved by grace through faith. Once you have received this gift of salvation, you will then walk in the light and favor of God's will for your life. If you stray away as I did completely, your heart will anguish the separation and nothing will satiate the emptiness you will feel. Also, living outside of God's grace which is what you do when you stray, puts you in danger of the evil one. Here is what I know to be true. Your heart is either given over to God where it will be renewed in His hands into a powerful love for His glory bringing you true happiness and meaning or your heart will be your own and it will deceive you all of your days. This will lead to misery and bitterness and ultimately destruction. Why? Because we, as humans, are unable to successfully guard our hearts against the evil one without God's protection. And once you receive salvation, you are no longer ignorant to your sin. Living in sin after salvation will turn your spirit away from God and creates a sad longing in your soul. Also, when you are saved, the Holy Spirit comes to dwell in your heart. Once you stray into a carnal existence, the Holy Spirit cannot stay. This opens the door for the devil. We open the door for the devil when we stray. We need God and trying to live without Him in our lives is like a fish trying to breathe air. It just won't work. And soon, if the fish doesn't give in to what is natural, he will die. A lot of people today receive their salvation and then at some point, they think they don't need God anymore. They think they got it covered. They put God on the back burner to call on when needed, like for example when someone gets sick and then they will pray. They don't pray otherwise and soon their relationship with God is starved. When you are starving, you will become delusional. You will start to change God's word to fit your lifestyle so there is no guilt. People deceive themselves through the influence of the devil. He will influence you to believe that everything is okay as long as you are basically a good person. Everything is okay as long as you sin in moderation. And don't call it sin. That is an ugly word. Let's refer to it as having some fun. Lighten up! Also, God is probably cool with your distant relationship with Him. He understands what you are going through. He understands that you have needs that you cannot control. He is grading on a curve. These simple lies that the devil feeds us, that we adopt as a way of life will destroy you. Here is the good news. It is never too late this side of eternity to realize our folly and come back to the flock!

A person can stray from God and spend their whole life blinded by their heart and live in helpless pain and confusion. A person can also decide to turn their heart over to God and spend their life in the light of his grace and abounding love. I lived most of my life in a black hole emotionally. Now that I have turned to God, my life is the mirror opposite. I could not be happier. I cannot even express in words the joy I feel on a daily basis. I float along in awe and gratitude. My life is not perfect but my heart is healed.

My mind is healthy and my soul is quenched. It doesn't matter what happens to me going forward.

Nothing can take away the peace that God grants. Everything I go through now has a completely different effect on me than it used to. I see things completely differently! I realize now that this life is so temporary. Nothing matters here. Not money, not things, not popularity, not even being in love. How free I am now that I get that! I watch TV and I could laugh at our society for how artificial it is. Except that it makes me sad. The devil is running rampant on Earth today. And he is having much success. But he has one less recently than he had before! I received salvation at a young age and then spent most of my adult life outside of God's grace. In other words, I got saved and then lived as if I was not. Oh the pain and waste I put myself through! I will spend the rest of my life having victory in Jesus as He intended. I will never own my heart again. I have willingly given it over to God and said "Take it, for it is yours". And He replied to me "I will take care of you, and you will never hunger again"

The Bible says in John 10:11-15:

> I am the good shepherd. The good shepherd lays down his life for the sheep. The hired hand is not the shepherd who owns the sheep. So when he sees the wolf coming, he abandons the sheep and runs away. Then the wolf attacks the flock and scatters it. The man runs away because he is a hired hand and cares nothing for the sheep. I am the good shepherd; I know my sheep and my sheep know me just as the Father knows me and I know the Father- and I lay down my life for the sheep.

The Bible says that the Lord is our shepherd and we as Christians are His sheep. The Lord guides His sheep along keeping them safe and happy. If there are one hundred sheep in the flock and they are all following Him like they should and one goes astray, God will chase after that one sheep relentlessly until it turns back. If it turns back, He will be more excited about the one than the ninety- nine that were following along the whole time. My story is about the one stray sheep. That is me. And I have a strong feeling, accompanied by God's revelation to me that you need to hear this. I believe there are more stray sheep out there than there are sheep that follow along exactly as they are supposed to do. Especially in this day and time with all the things we have now to distract us. I spent most of my life straying and I want people to understand what straying will cost you. When you are born, God has a plan for your life. When you stray, not only do you interrupt the blessings God had in store for you but you also put yourself in danger. Most importantly, your heart is forever troubled. I want people to understand that God will chase you relentlessly until the end- out of love! He loves you. We don't even deserve God's love and yet He loves us beyond what I can even describe. He will chase you until you turn to Him and when you do, He is waiting with open arms and this mercy I speak of along with a love you never could have imagined in your wildest dreams! So here is my story...

MY HISTORY

MY HISTORY

I was born on a Friday night in Japan in 1971. My dad was drafted during the Vietnam War and sent there where my mother joined him later. As soon as she got there, she got pregnant with me by accident. She had me there, in a naval hospital, and then returned to the States six weeks later. Both my parents have told me I was an accident. Don't ever tell your children that. Even if it is true, just don't. Focus on the positive when telling children their history. The seeds you plant early run deep. And they harvest esteem. Having said that, I love my parents dearly. They always did their very best. And I have a large family of wonderful people who have loved me my whole life and spoiled me immensely. But one of the lies I started believing my whole life is that I was a mistake- not an accident, a mistake. That is a very painful thought born from a very powerful word. Do I blame my parents for this? Of course not! And the more I submit to God's will in my life and live in obedience to Him, the more God reveals all the lies the devil has ever presented to me as lies and they become nothing to me. However, I think that we, as humans, should understand our vulnerability to words and only use them to build people up. You know the old saying that actions speak louder than words? I couldn't disagree with that statement more! I think words are very powerful. Otherwise, why would I let something like that statement haunt me growing up and discard the fact that my mother took care of me and loved me? I don't think people realize how powerful words really are. The Bible tells us the tongue is a fire. This basically means that our mouths have a way of getting us into trouble. Your words actually have the power to make you physically sick but they can also make you strong .That is why preachers are always telling us Christians to read the Bible and digest its words. Because to feed our spirit with God's Word, literally, changes our hearts. His word is the truth. His word is infallible. If we fill our minds with the truth, our hearts will grow strong. Have you ever met someone who never had anything good to say? Everything out of their mouths was either poor mouthing their situation or judging someone for the way they looked or dressed. Or maybe the person had a foul mouth and the only thing out of it was curse words. Did you ever notice that person had a miserable life situation and that most people didn't want to be around them? Try to picture words coming out of your mouth in a visible smoke that flows through the air. That smoke flows away from your body and envelopes the area. Those around you are surrounded by it. Negativity through the mouth is like a virus that spreads and affects others. If everyone took that seriously, people would not talk so much! On the other hand, words spilled out through love touch others in the way God intended them too. Think about the people you come into contact with every day. Maybe the only person you come into contact with today is someone in line with you at the post office. The words you choose to share with that person can leave an impression that changes their whole way of thinking. It can be scary but we do have that kind of power with our words. James 3:6 says:

> The tongue also is a fire, a world of evil among the parts of the body. It corrupts the whole person, sets the whole course of his life on fire, and is itself set on fire by hell.

Now, the devil waits patiently biding his time to destroy. He is nothing if he isn't patient. I think the first and biggest weapon in his arsenal is words. A person's mind can be infiltrated with painful lies created from someone's words and then it can be carried around as the truth in the heart. This is why it so important to understand what God's salvation means for us because the devil starts his attack on a person early in life. And perception is a person's truth. Let me say that again. Perception is a person's truth. The devil will attack your perception because he knows it is a human's most vulnerable spot. He is not stupid. He knows what works! I have learned that the Bible tells us that we are wonderfully and fearfully made in the womb. Jeremiah 1:5 says:

> *Before I formed you in the womb knew you, before you were born I set you apart...*

God fashions each one of us in a special way in His image. Genesis 1:27 says:

> *So God created man in his own image, in the image of God he created him; male and female he created them.*

So everyone is here for a reason, for His reason and everyone is beautiful. I get that now. How much pain and time did that cost me in the meantime? How much did the devil sit back and laugh at me? This is not my parent's fault. This is a result of having no defense toward the devil. We are helpless to fight the devil without God and Satan will try to destroy you. It is his singular mission.

I grew up an only child which I thought was great. I never had to share anything. Everything under the Christmas tree was for me! When you are an only child, you grow up very independent and as a result, as an adult, you don't need social interaction as much as the next guy. In fact, I love my alone time. I cherish it. I am ashamed to admit that more often I prefer my own company to that of anyone else. And I need time to myself on a regular basis. Without it, I can get cranky! As an only child and the first grandchild, I was smothered with love from my whole family. My first clear memory is standing under the kitchen table in my grandmother's kitchen and peeking out at her legs as she was talking to me. She was telling me that I was getting ready to start kindergarten and that I was a big girl now. I remember how excited I was. I was blessed with a grandmother who had a heart that could hold the ocean. I loved her more than words will ever be able to express. But her love for me surpassed my own love for her. She shaped my heart until she passed away in August of 1999. I was twenty-eight years old. I thought I wasn't ready or prepared to live in this world without her. I have since realized that she made sure I was before she left. My grandmother never went to church that I ever saw but she was still one of the most influential people in my life. She loved me in a way that burns in my heart to this day. When a person loves you with that kind of unconditional love, it is a peek into the kind of love Jesus has for us. So for me, she was a major example to me of God's love just through the kind of love she showed me and everyone around her. That stayed with me and when I wallowed in periods of deep depression, I believe her love helped me to survive. I don't even think it was on a conscience level. I think you can plant seeds in people. These seeds harvest a tree that roots itself into someone's soul. So she has been gone for twelve years and I am only beginning to scratch the surface of the monumental way her love has affected me and shaped my heart. The Bible tells us that the second greatest commandment is that we should love our neighbor as ourselves. In the book of Matthew, a Pharisee asks Jesus what is the greatest commandment. He answers in chapter 22 verses 37-40:

> Jesus replied: Love the Lord your God with all your heart, and with all your soul, and with all your mind. This is the first and greatest commandment. And the second is like it: Love your neighbor as yourself. All the Law and the Prophets hang on these two commandments.

So before I even understood God's greatest commandments, I was being shaped by them. She was my favorite person and I think that anyone who ever knew her felt the same way. Her smile would light up a room and her blue eyes always danced. She was funny and beautiful but never knew it. She had a deep profound effect on my life and looking back, I know that she had no idea that her love, her life would be instrumental and key to another. She is only one of many people God chose to put in my life who surrounded me with love. So my childhood was mostly normal and happy. My parents were only nineteen when I came along so they were very young raising a child. We lived right beside my grandparents and they were like parents to me. I was always at their house. They always told people I was their fourth daughter. And my mom's sisters were much like older sisters to me rather than aunts. Still are. I have always been very close to them. My mother was born December 22, 1951, the first of three girls. As a teenager, my mother grew up to be a speed skater who was ranked fourth in the country. She is so beautiful. Her skin is flawless. I have a picture of her in Japan pregnant with me and she looks like a young Elizabeth Taylor. I have always been proud of my mother. She dances to the beat of her own drum. I have always admired her intelligence the most. My mother is a very street-smart person who always remains stable and copes with problems using sheer will power. She amazes me.

SMALL TOWN

SMALL TOWN

I grew up in a small town in the South. Until I turned nine, we lived in a small yellow house beside my grandparents. At that time, my mother was a hair dresser as they used to be called and my dad sold insurance. That was back when the insurance agents literally went from house to house to collect premiums. More often than not, my dad would pay for someone's premium out of his own pocket because the person could not afford to. Neither could we! My dad used to race motorcycles back then and there was always a lot of his biker friends hanging out at our house. Everyone was nice to me. I remember one of them gave me a puppy one day. You never forget people who give you pets. My dad had plenty of friends back then but this one guy sticks in my memory. I don't even remember what he looked like. I just remember the copper colored puppy he gave me that I called Red. I think it is important to keep in mind that as humans we affect each other with our behavior towards each other. God calls us to love one another and I believe the reason it is so important is because when you have love coming at you from different sources, it will stack up like food for the winter. Like I have said before, I was unequipped for many years against Satan but I believe the good people here on Earth who have influenced me or prayed for me brought me through. So I don't think we should ever underestimate the small ways we show people love. And I am not talking about your spouse or your immediate family or friends. Although it is important to treat these people with love, I feel that it is even more important to reach out to people outside of your immediate circle. The smallest gesture can affect someone.

That also goes for small gestures of anger or rudeness. Think of the brain as a tape recorder and the heart as a flower. A person's brain basically records all events in their lives, everything they consciously experience. It records the good along with the bad. Then the event is sent to the flower where it either waters it or withers it. All events do this and as you can imagine, person to person experiences will ultimately have the most profound effects. If you are in a car wreck and injured slightly, you will heal from the experience after some time. But if you have someone speak to you in an abusive or cruel way, it will engrave itself into memory. I know it is true because we get upset even if we have a confrontation with a complete stranger. That conversation will literally stay with us for months. And you know if something like that stays on the tip of your tongue for that kind of time, it is permanently on our tape recorder even if on the surface, we forget about it. That is because we get our feelings hurt. You can call it whatever you want to. You can call it ego, temper, or dignity- it still boils down to our feelings. And the problem with hurting someone's feelings is this: you run the risk of setting that person up for Satan's schemes. I can remember being very small and playing in my great grandmother's back yard. She would have white sheets hung out on the line to dry. I would run through the middle of them and I could smell the fresh clean scent. That memory is there forever in a good way. The flower grows. I also remember my dad singing "You are my sunshine" to me all the time as a kid. That is a great memory locked in my heart forever. The flower grows and blooms. Having my ex-husband call me profane words because I did not wash his socks- damaging. This is because even though I knew deep down that he was wrong, Satan chimed in. I began to believe that I was unworthy of anything better than that. So the flower withers. Be careful how you treat people. And also remember that when someone treats you unfairly, the best revenge is quick forgiveness. This disarms Satan and his plan before he gets a foothold and changes your destiny. Not the person who hurt you, your destiny. I want to say something on forgiveness for a second. When you decide to forgive someone who has hurt you, this action is between you and God. All of our actions are indeed between us and the Lord. If you think of it that way, it may be easier to understand that forgiveness is vital. In life, we should always strive to do what we know is the right thing to do because ultimately, we answer to God for every decision. We do not answer for others. That is comforting in itself to realize that when someone hurts you, they will answer for it. You may not be there as you would like to be to witness it of course but that doesn't matter. We need to take comfort in the fact that people answer for the wrong they do in this life. This should also make us realize that we too will be held accountable for our actions. 2 Corinthians 5:10 says:

> For we must all appear before the judgment seat of Christ, that each one may receive what is due him for the things done while in the body, whether good or bad.

I find it interesting that every time I am about to do something that is wrong, I immediately feel the Lord moving in my spirit and giving me clear discernment. I sometimes will start to justify what I am doing in my head and I have noticed that discerning voice in my head will slowly disappear. There will be a residual feeling that it is wrong that leaves me feeling lousy. As Christians, the Holy Spirit dwells in our hearts and as such, He moves our hearts in the direction of what is right and wrong. You can tune it out if you want to but it is there. People who have never been saved do not have this beautiful gift but instead rely on their own moral conclusions. Well, what is wrong with that? The problem is that people are not holy by nature. We are sinful. So even though the vast majority of society would agree that murder is wrong and most people do not murder, those same people will find justification for "lesser" sins such as greed, vanity, and fornication. Let's face it. There are reality shows on TV right now that glamorize women who pose nude for a living. People try to justify sinful behavior because deep down they think it should be ok because it satisfies a carnal desire. Sin is so entrenched in our very skin that the things of the flesh rule one's mind. Sex feels good during the act so people think it should be okay outside of marriage. The problem with this type of thinking is that people do not conceive of the holiness of God. He is completely removed from carnal thinking and is wholly and completely perfect. Our sin, even that which we enjoy, is so ugly in the sight of God that it grieves Him and He must bring judgment down upon it. Once you get a grip on how wrong your sin really is, I believe then you can begin to contemplate your actions each day as to whether or not they would please God. I think we should cherish the gift of knowing with certainty what is right and what is wrong. The more I study God's word and spend time in prayer, I notice the clearer His truth becomes. I have also noticed that when the truth becomes clear, if I choose to listen, how glad my heart becomes. He will actually fill me with a joyful emotion as a result of listening to His guidance. It is a small victory and I rejoice every time I actually listen and do the right thing. You may think that doing the right thing may leave you longing for the wrong thing you contemplated. Actually, I have experienced the most peace inside when I have listened to God. Over the course of a day I have multiple chances to decide to do the right thing. Every time the answer is so simple but so often the action is such a battle. Sometimes I choose right and sometimes I choose wrong. One thing is true. I have never regretted doing the right thing. I spend a lot of time in sorrow over all the wrongs. You would think experience would teach us that making right choices would just be simpler! But the truth is that it will always be a battle and that is why we need God's guidance and strength. I do have days that are more successful than others.

Christians are a work in progress. The important thing to remember is that we must strive to live as Jesus did with the understanding that we will never achieve holy while we are here on Earth. Listen closely and you will feel Jesus' love guiding you more and more over time. And here is a good rule of thumb. Anytime you start to contemplate what you are about to do or say, you should realize this is a red flag! If you find yourself justifying your behavior to the voice in your head, this is your warning that you are having a conversation with the Almighty and telling him why you think he is wrong. It is rebellion and God is trying to spare you from yourself! Proverbs 3:18 says:

She is a tree of life to those who embrace her; those who lay hold of her will be blessed.

The "she" in this verse refers to wisdom and those who seek it are promised a long healthy and prosperous life here on Earth. Seeking this wisdom has nothing to do with educating ourselves and everything to do with obedience to God. Once we stop fooling ourselves about our sin, we can understand its true consequences. At that point, we can discover a healthy fear of the Lord and in turn repent from our sin. Only then can we start to live in obedience to God's commands which are clearly laid out for us in the Bible. As we begin to walk in the light, God will grant us wisdom and a deeper knowledge of Him.

The first time I ever went to church was when I was about six years old. A friend invited me and my mother let me go. I think I went more than once and I can remember wearing a brown corduroy skirt with cowboy boots each time I went because we were poor at the time. Eventually some friends of my parents invited them to church and soon we were going together. My parents got involved in Sunday school teaching and church became a regular thing for us. At that young age, I could remember that there had been life for me before church and then there was my new church life. I did not feel like I understood a lot. The other kids there had been going to church for their whole lives and I could tell they knew more factually about the Bible than I did. I didn't even know how to pray properly.

Sometimes I could hear the other kids at church making fun of me for the way I prayed when asked to pray aloud. I definitely felt like an outcast however, my feelings for God were strong and I loved the preacher. I do remember God's presence in my heart. I was baptized when I was nine years old. I was so young that I had not even fully grasped the concept of Jesus so it was paramount that I stopped going at the time I did which was somewhere around the age of twelve. My parents had had a problem with something the church did and didn't agree and we stopped going. I can remember my mother taking me with her to visit some other churches but we never found anything that felt like home. Pretty soon, we completely stopped going. Even though

I have always felt God has protected me since I spent that small time in church early on, I realize that not going in my teens was detrimental to my decision making for the future. I was vulnerable to Satan because I was not in the Word, not in prayer, not in church. I was basically like a new little lamb that fell behind because she was too young to keep up and strayed away. Being so young, I did not grasp that I was straying. I was just a kid and one minute we were in church and the next minute, we were not. I knew that I loved God at twelve years old but at that age, I had not even started reading the Bible. I knew the basic story of Jesus dying for my sins and raising from the dead to ascend to Heaven so that I could have eternal life. Got that. But I was too young to realize that with salvation comes a life journey of walking with God and growing as a Christian from one level to another through Bible study and prayer. And I did not realize that God followed me right off the path and stayed beside me waiting for the chance to direct me back to the flock.

I realize now that God had a plan for my life even at the age of nine. When I veered off the path, meaning that I stopped walking with God, His plan for me was sidetracked and the devil got his foothold. You see Satan also had a plan for my life. He did not start a full attack until I was in my twenties. But he did start deceiving me which laid a foundation for his future schemes. Getting side tracked is kind of like going on vacation and getting lost on the way. Everything is great and you have your course all mapped out. You are excited about where you are heading. You begin your journey probably singing along to the radio and grinning as you bounce along the open highway with philosophical thoughts running through your head. Something happens along the way and you become sidetracked. Maybe you wanted to take a short cut or maybe you saw a sign for hot doughnuts and you knew you didn't need those doughnuts but hey, you are on vacation right? So before you know it, you are lost. You are not even sure how it happened. The first emotion to set in is anxiety followed by anger and a nagging helpless feeling. Your journey goes from being a fun filled adventure to a painful and emotional ride that you just wish would end. You will eventually reach your destination if you don't give up however; it will cost you time, energy, and happiness. It will steal your joy. It is the same way with God's plan for our lives. He has a divine plan for all his children. Whether you believe that or not is unimportant. It is a fact. We were created on purpose by the creator with the purpose of having a relationship with Him and glorifying Him with our lives. How many people actually do that? The plan is sidetracked! Our lives are a series of choices and attitudes. Every decision we make is either based on God's divine plan for us, emotion, or the devil's influence. Our attitude is created the same way. If you become sidetracked, your life will take on a whole different path than God intended. How sad. The good news is that at any point, as long as your heart is still beating and he hasn't returned to Earth, He can lift you up and put you back on His path once you give your heart to Him and submit to His will. He will then still fill your life with peace and joy.

Ephesians 2:8-10 says:

> *For it is by grace you have been saved, through faith-*
> *and this not from yourselves, it is the gift of God- not*
> *by works, so that no one can boast. For we are God's*
> *workmanship, created in Christ Jesus to do good works,*
> *which God prepared in advance for us to do.*

Because God saves us when our sin deems us unworthy, we should spend the rest of our lives praising God and witnessing to others who haven't heard the Gospel. Our job is to win souls for Christ. Early in a person's life, the devil will try to turn someone's focus onto themselves and away from others, away from God. If he is successful, then he sidetracks a person's destiny. He can accomplish this in different ways. He can persuade someone to spend all of their time getting rich. He can persuade someone to spend all their time trying to look good. He can persuade someone to spend all their time feeling sorry for themselves. The devil will zero in on the thing that someone is vulnerable to since we are all different and have different weaknesses. We all have different strengths too so where I could care less about money, I struggle with vanity. If the devil can turn your focus away from God early and convince you in whatever manner to put it on yourself, he has laid his foundation for destruction. This is because a life focused on self leads to waste. Waste over time leads to loss of purpose and loss of purpose leads to death. If you don't believe the devil holds this kind of power, let me clarify. We have all watched the movie based on a true story of the model that starts out with such promise and ends up committing suicide. What went wrong? The girl is completely focused on herself right off the bat. She is young and beautiful and has her whole life ahead of her. The modeling world brings her into contact with the wrong kinds of people and all kinds of temptation. Pretty soon she is doing drugs and then she loses herself and before she knows what has happened, she is on the edge of the abyss. She suffers from erratic emotions and thinks she has nothing to live for. Once a person becomes involved in something sinful, they allow the devil to gain a foothold. This means the devil slips into a person's heart and attacks them through their mind and destroys their soul. In other words, the model started out as a small town naive girl who just wanted to be "somebody". Her weakness is that she is someone who desires attention and has a problem with self- esteem. The devil, who is sniffing around the flock at all times looking for prey, sees this girl and pounces. She starts believing it's okay to do drugs to help her keep her weight down and distracts her from God. Then once drugs takes over her will, she slips into someone she no longer recognizes in the mirror. Her cup gets knocked over and her soul spills out and evaporates away. There is nothing left but an empty shell full of loneliness and shame. At the moment she reaches her darkest point, her thoughts become "you are worthless. Why don't you just give up? There is no comfort coming for you." She is so far outside God's grace, she can't even feel His presence and she kills herself. The danger in believing that the devil is powerless in our lives is that when he starts his attack, you don't realize where it comes from. You believe that all of your negative thoughts come from yourself and therefore you nurture those thoughts. The Bible tells us the devil is the Father of all lies. All negative thoughts come from the devil. Being properly equipped with this truth, which comes from God's Word, allows a person to ignore or rebuke all negative thoughts before they catch us unaware. I believe that Satan's strategy is always subtle and always well planned out, patient and smart. Think about all the friends you personally know who die too young. The devil convinces people that they should spend life partying and having fun. They are fooled into believing that drugs won't hurt them but instead will make them feel like they are powerful. They begin to ignore the nagging feeling they have that God wouldn't approve. They tell themselves that they only live once and to take advantage of their youth. Then he kills them. I believe there are many doors that Satan can enter through. I believe the most common is attacking a person's self -esteem. If he can get inside your head and make you believe that you are fat or ugly or dumb or different, he can gain a foothold. This is why it is imperative that we love everyone and treat all people as worthy. Once a person buys into what the devil is selling, he can then use his arsenal to begin an attack on this person's life. The person is vulnerable in their pain and he will convince them to obsess on their wrong thoughts. This will then lead to self- destructive behavior. Bringing a person to misery is the devil's battle plan. Once a person is brought to a state of misery and doesn't know how to turn to God, the devil can plan his attacks through a variety of sins. I used to party all the time to excess. Excess was not a result of the fun I was having. It was the only way I knew how to numb the pain and confusion I lived in. I was miserable and the devil had convinced me that this self-destructive behavior was my only escape. All misery has a source. That source is Lucifer, the fallen angel. He hates all of God's children and wants nothing more than to steal your joy, kill your relationship with God and ultimately, destroy your very life. I believe the main routes of self-destructive behavior are sex outside of marriage, adultery, drugs, alcohol, hatred, vanity, greed, envy and narcissism. Why? Because all of these things are contrary to God's heart and they are completely accepted by our society. Because they are acceptable in society, it gives the devil free reign to use these sins as a door to enter a person's soul. Then he can work on destroying your marriage, your health, your life. If you think you can engage in a sinful lifestyle and "handle" it, you are blinded by pride. Pride is the devil's secret weapon. When you puff out your chest, you expose your heart to the devil's intentions. If you are irritated by any of this, God is speaking to you right now. He is dealing with you and you better pay attention. God's intention is that we have life and have it abundantly. He is never the source of misery. He loves us and wishes for us peace and joy.

Psalm 119:105 says:

Your word is a lamp to my feet and a light for my path.

This verse is to me the most obvious indicator that the Bible should be read by us on a daily basis. His word is the truth and will clearly give you the tools and rules on how to live your life in a way that is pleasing to Him.

Ecclesiastes 12:1 says:

Remember your Creator in the days Of your youth, before the days Of trouble come and the years approach when you will say, 'I find no pleasure in them'.

This verse is a great warning about straying. It amazes me how much simpler my life could have been up until now had I read the Bible! It is precious and priceless. Instead, I just made up my rules as I went. What a disaster! People fall into the very wrong thinking that a person should just try to live a basically good life and not hurt others and that is enough. Not even close my friends! Don't fool yourselves into believing that you run the show and that you have the wisdom, without God, how to do so. You have no wisdom! The beginning of wisdom is fear of the Lord. Out of the heart of man is born malice, greed, envy, murder. We are born into sin so anything we produce solely is or will turn to evil. If you try to walk through life without Jesus in your heart, you will focus on yourself, your needs, your wants, and your desires and it will bring you down. While this is happening, the devil, whom you will not recognize because you cannot properly discern him, will lead you to believe that you are doing fine and then soon he will encourage you to repay evil to those who hurt you and to hold a grudge. He will persuade you that you have to look out for number one because you are after all wise and talented. He will make you believe that you should not trust others and that you should spend your life on earthly goals. He will then persuade you to believe that most sin is okay in this day and age and that as long as you are not hurting anyone or going to jail, you are fine. He will convince you that everyone is doing what you are doing. Well he is right about the last statement. Matthew 7:13-14 tells us:

> Enter through the narrow gate. For wide is the gate and broad is the road that leads to destruction, and many enter through it. But small is the gate and narrow the road that leads to life and only a few find it.

If you read this verse and you feel a fearful tug in your heart, don't choose to ignore it. Life is so short here and you never know when your time is up. Matthew 7:21 says:

> Not everyone who says to me, 'Lord, Lord,' will enter the kingdom of Heaven, but only he who does the will of my Father who is in heaven.

Now read Galatians 5:22-23 which says:

> But the fruit of the Spirit is love, joy, peace, patience, kindness, goodness, faithfulness, gentleness and self-control.

Once you completely put your focus on seeking a relationship with our Lord and getting to know Him, once you completely submit to His will and surrender your life to Him, your life will take on wings like eagles. Your mind will become clear on what is right and wrong. You will hate sin where before you reveled in it. Your heart will begin to love all people where before you didn't even love yourself. Your life will take on purpose where before you battled through each day. Joy will replace misery and peace will replace hurt. I was once lost and now

I am found. I clawed through life depressed and suicidal. Now I soar through life with a happiness that literally cannot be put into words. My God fills me up in a way that is unattainable with any other thing on Earth. People spend their whole lives seeking happiness in every way known to man except by the one who started it all. My only grief in life now is the knowledge that a person's will is stubborn. I write this because I lived outside of God's grace for so long and experienced all the world had to offer. In it, my heart never felt any peace. My life was never right. Now I have everything and I want to share this so I pray for those who need God and I give thanks that he followed His sheep for so far and so long. His mercy during my sin and His patience during my rebellion amaze me every time I think on it. I will spend the rest of my life walking with God in obedience to His commands and seeking to please Him. He waited on me, a sinner, He followed me, and He gently turned me in His direction. He forgave my sin and surrounded me with His loving and holy light. I will spend eternity with Him because He never gave up on me. I aspire to please Him with every breath. I long to glorify Him with my life. Thank you Father God for loving me.

THE GOOD YEARS

THE GOOD YEARS

By the time I was twelve, we were living in a suburban neighborhood about a mile and a half from my grandmother's neighborhood. I remember thinking this was a very long way! My dad would soon go into the car business where his income would begin to head straight upward. At the same time, my mother was starting nursing school and our financial picture would soon leave our humble beginnings behind. My dad purchased a bass fishing boat and both parents drove nice vehicles. My dad went from racing motorcycles to playing golf. Times were good. This was the early eighties. I had met my first "best" friend. I loved my new neighborhood because there were a lot of kids my age to play with. I grew up in the good old days when parents did not have to worry about their children being abducted. We would go deep into the woods and spend hours or walk to the fire department or roller skate all over the town. I just knew to come home before dark. That was the big thing, "before dark". If you came home after dark, you were in big trouble. I would never leave my son unattended in the back yard these days but back then, it was a different world. Looking back, it was certainly the best time of my life! We would dredge through the school year just trying to make it until summer vacation. Then we had three months to just play! And back then, your parents would let you stay home while they worked. Kids were different back then and didn't get into trouble. We just played. We kids had our own society. We even had our own mode of transportation. I personally drove a skateboard. The leader of our group drove a BMX bike. So every morning, I would hop on my skateboard and head for the leader's house.

Incidentally, that was across the road and two houses down. After everyone eventually arrived, we would decide on the agenda for the day. It was a little like Lord of the Flies meets The Little Rascals. There was a lot of power struggling going on in our group for Alpha male and female. But there was also a lot of childish mayhem! Our leader, and rightfully so, was a science fanatic and very intelligent. I heard he grew up to be an engineer which sounds about right. He was always building something or conducting an experiment. He was a little bossy like me but without him, the ideas we came up with would have never made it to fruition. I remember one summer we decided to make soap boxes to drive. The old- fashioned kind you steer with your feet. Our fearless leader made five of them using old lawnmower tires and string and wood. Some were even two seaters. After completion, we promptly started racing them down the biggest hill in the neighborhood. Eventually, someone had the bright idea to hook them all together like a train and race downhill at top speed! Well, I used my talent for persuasion, which was crafted to perfection even at age twelve to convince the group that I should drive the train. You can imagine how this went down. Oh, it was great for most of the way. That is until I decided to make a sharp left -hand turn. The entire train rolled over and dragged us the rest of the way down. We were bloody but we were laughing and regaling the story to each other with much enthusiasm and exaggeration as we took turns washing off our battered knees by the hose pipe. I still have the scars on my knees to prove that day. Those were the days I will never forget and I think most people would probably agree that the time period after age ten to just before puberty is the best. Life is the most uncomplicated it is ever going to be. Friends are the most important they are ever going to be. And I will say that a person has their whole life ahead of them.

I felt a pull to go to church in my teens but I ignored it because, well, I was a teenager and all that implies! In the ninth grade, I discovered quite by accident that I was a natural long- distance runner with an incredible talent. I say I discovered it by accident because I had joined the track team in the seventh grade when I was twelve only because my friend did. I ran sprint events in the seventh and eighth grades and usually came in last. I didn't even care. I was not competitive. I just had fun with my friends. In the ninth grade, during one particular track meet, my coach came to me and told me I would be running the mile event. I told her I could not possibly even finish a mile. She told me she didn't have enough girls and that I had to. I got so upset I starting crying and told her if she made me run the event, I would quit the team. She said I could quit after the race. So I ran it and won it. I thought to myself "well, ok, I have happened on to something here!" I remember that it was easy! I wasn't even out of breath. My dad was so excited and told me I had a "God given" talent. After that day, I always ran the long-distance events in track and always went undefeated. In high school, I ran the mile and two mile and I also joined the cross-country team. I had finally found something that I not only could do but I could do it better than anyone else! That was a huge boost to my self-esteem. It gave me identity which I already was desperately craving. I spent my high school years as a "good girl" who just played sports and got along with everyone. I was smart but my grades were average. That was fine at home as long as my running was first priority. My dad really got caught up in it believing that I was destined for the Olympics. The problem was that I never dreamed that dream. And if you don't want something for yourself, it is not going to happen. And I was fine with my accomplishments in high school. I received Athlete of the Year in my senior year in high school. I also got a scholarship to run in college. I ran in the nationals in college. After that, running lost its magic for me. I was always under so much pressure to win that it zapped the fun out of it and became a burden for me. I jog now and it is all the joy it should have been back then. So in college, I tried out for the tennis team and made it as a walk on! The first year I proved myself and came back the next year with a scholarship for tennis. By my senior year in college, I was playing first seed. I did not win matches like I won races but I loved it! I loved being on a team and not having the pressure to win all the time. So early in life, I had a real gift that came from the Lord. I knew that I did, that much was obvious. But the only time I prayed about it was during competition. So did God have another plan for me in regards to the running? I will never know. Maybe He planned to use me at age nine and I will never know that either. After graduation, I moved to Florida with my best friend. So here I am, a girl with a four -year degree, a reputation for being a great athlete and a "good girl", and my whole life ahead of me. Why did I suddenly feel like I was at my end?

Well the devil will try to destroy your life. If you don't believe that, you are in a very dangerous place.

Like I have said before, it is when we don't realize the devil's power on earth that he will come after us.

And if we are not walking with God, we are like the gazelle. She is so beautiful, graceful, and helpless. The tiger will slowly creep up, patiently watching and waiting and making sure she is vulnerable. Then without warning he will attack and kill. The gazelle never saw it coming and by the time she did, it was too late. He devours her. He takes her life and she is no more. I was that gazelle. I had been out of church all through my teens so I had not built any kind of guard up against the devil. My relationship with God was nonexistent. Oh, I would have told you I was a Christian back then if you had asked me. But I had no proof to back it up. I am so disappointed in myself for saying that for so many years and being wrong. And I hear people say it all the time now and it reminds me. People will say stuff like "No, I don't go to church, you don't have to be in church to be a Christian" or "l don't really believe in the Bible but yes I am a Christian" or my favorite is "I don't think I believe in Hell but I know there is a Heaven" You cannot pick and choose what feels good! And people don't "believe" in Hell because they are hoping it doesn't exist! Well, God tells us that it is every bit as real as Heaven when He says in Ezekiel 26:20-21:

> *...then I will bring you down with those who go down to the pit, to the people of long ago. I will make you dwell in the Earth below, as in ancient ruins, with those who go down to the pit, and you will not return or take your place in the land of the living. I will bring you to a horrible end and you will be no more. You will be sought, but you will never again be found, declares the Sovereign Lord.*

And if you are really a Christian you will want to go to church because in church you have the opportunity to worship and praise our Lord openly and fellowship with other believers. Also, the Holy Spirit resides in the church and going there puts you in the presence of God. A Christian craves the presence of the Lord. And once you are saved you become part of the body of Christ which is the church. And for people who don't believe in the Bible I don't even know what to say. If you don't believe in the Bible, you don't believe in God because it was written in divine inspiration from God Himself and every word in it is God breathed. 2 Timothy 3:16-17 says:

> *All scripture is God-breathed and is useful for teaching, rebuking, correcting, and training in righteousness, so that the man of God may be thoroughly equipped for every good work.*

God also says to us in Revelation 22:18-19:

> *I warn everyone who hears the words Of the prophecy of this book: If anyone adds anything to them, God will add to him the plagues described in this book. And if anyone takes words away from this book Of prophecy, God will take away from him his share in the tree of life and in the holy city, which are described in this book.*

In other words, the Bible contains everything you need to know about God, His laws, Jesus, how to receive salvation, and finally how to live as a Christian. Anyone arrogant enough to say they don't believe in it is deceiving themselves. Even the devil believes in the Bible. He quoted scripture to Jesus when he was tempting Him in the desert. You either believe it all or you believe none of it. I think that people who say they only believe parts of it are copping out to their own sin. They are comforting themselves with a denial blanket. It is kind of like wishful thinking. Well, I won't think about how I am living and it will just go away. Do not deceive yourself right into Hell! As I was saying, I had no relationship with Jesus. I can remember visiting church occasionally through the years and feeling nothing. I had strayed far away into the wilderness and did not know how to find my way back. The devil had waited patiently and now he attacked me around the age of twenty. My parents had just split up and my world fell apart. Now keep in mind that if I had been walking with the Lord when this occurred, I could have taken this to God in prayer and He would have carried me through it to the other side. Because I was not walking with God, I tried to comfort myself. To make things worse, I moved to Florida and away from all of my family. I was not emotionally strong enough to do this at this time but I did not know that until I got there. Sometimes I look back and wonder what God would have done with my life had I been walking with Him at age twenty. I have to remind myself that the past is no longer important because it is gone and He is using me now. We should never sit around regretting the past. We should be grateful that we have a future. Besides, regret is another tool of the devil. Anyway, I was living in Florida with my best friend. Florida is beautiful and the weather is fantastic. I was young and healthy and had everything in front of me. This is the first time in my life I started considering suicide. At twenty, the devil had convinced me that my life was a waste and that I would feel broken forever. I felt like I could not to share these thoughts with anyone because such thoughts were irrational and I was crazy. My parents had split up and I was devastated and confused. Confusion is of the devil. He uses confusion to gain a foothold. In my confusion, I felt great pain. My heart was broken. I kind of held it together in front of my friend. I know she picked up on my erratic behavior and mood swings but she was out of town a lot on her job. I think she may have worried about me without knowing what to do since she did witness some of my self-destructive behavior. This is when I first started sleeping around and abusing alcohol. Now whenever my friend was around, we would work out together and play tennis. I was witty and charming. But the bomb was ticking just below the surface and I felt like I was screaming all the time but no one could hear me. I began having constant conversations with myself about how I should be ashamed of myself because I was worthless. I told myself that everyone knew I was trash and that no man would ever love me. I also started believing that my parents didn't love me anymore. I was convinced that I had been forgotten and in my confusion and pain, I felt invisible. Unfortunately, the feeling of being invisible is one that I have struggled with over the years. Satan knows this is a personal weakness of mine and he pounces on it every time he gets the chance. Now whenever I start to feel that way, I pray about it and realize that it is a feeling, not a reality. Sometimes I laugh when I think that a single thought in my mind was able to bring me into such destruction merely because I entertained it! When the feeling surfaces now, I am able to use the strength and wisdom God has granted me to purge the thought before it takes root. I have been doing that for a while now and it does not have near the power it used to! I think the biggest lie the devil sold me was that I was on some level mentally ill because my paternal grandfather had been schizophrenic. I really bought into that and spent most of my time angry and confused. I felt lost. I felt completely alone. The devil convinced me I was all alone! I had aunts and uncles, grandparents, parents, my best friend, and yet I was all alone! Satan always kept me from reaching out to any of these folks in a real way so my torment stayed inside me. I was in too much pain to even understand that. I know that during this time God had His merciful hand on my life because I am still here. I did things that I should have died from and I entertained thoughts of suicide too much. I look back and it scares me that my thoughts were on suicide more than any other thing! God intervened concerning that or I would not still be here to write this. I never actually tried because had I tried, I would have succeeded. I kept those thoughts a secret. Twice I decided to cash in and both times, a friend walked in on me. Neither time did either friend know they had walked in on me counting out the pills, but their very presence was enough to snap me out of it. Thank you Father God for always showing mercy. God mercifully followed me during this time as I went further and further from the flock. You see there are no accidents and no luck concerning God's grace. He decided He wanted me around and that my future held a fruitful life in Him. So He kept my life in His hands. Praise you Jesus, my Father.

People walk around unhappy, unfulfilled, confused and without purpose. They ruin their lives and their relationships and they don't understand why. Then they dig deeper and deeper into the pit of destruction with seemingly no way out. What is not understood is that God sent His only son Jesus to Earth to die for our sins so that we may have salvation. Once you accept Jesus as your savior and turn your heart to God, He will mend your heart and fill you with peace and joy.

You cannot run your own life. You must surrender it to God. Let Him guide you and you will experience true happiness. Ignore Him and you will only experience disappointment, sorrow, and pain. We were not created to run our own lives. It is not natural and it won't work. We need God's guidance to keep us safe from the devil gaining a foothold. Also, with God, we have power over the devil. We are no longer at his mercy. We are not freed from temptation but we are no longer bound to sin. We become lions in a field of mice. And with God, you will experience victory in your life and find your purpose. You are a child of God and as such, born with a purpose through Him for your life. Imagine where we would be if we let God run our lives and hearts from the beginning of our journey. Where would we be? What heights would we soar? His power is limitless. We limit God's intent with our stubborn will and lack of faith. Instead of being obedient to God's commands and loving Him over everything else, we lead our own lives and never even ask his opinion. The famous song that Elvis sang called "I did it my way" sums up all of humanity. We think we know what is important and we kid ourselves that God "sympathizes" with our lifestyle choices. Then our lives eventually become a train wreck and we are surprised? At this point, a lot of people will then actually blame God for their situation. God doesn't cause problems. He doesn't punish people for their wrong choices. God walks beside you every day, a friend, waiting and hoping to talk to you. His ear is open every time we pray. Our lack of faith suspends His power over our lives. If you really believe that God cannot help you with your tiny little problem, you are looking at God with binoculars turned around the wrong way. I say tiny problem because anything you have is tiny in respect to God. God created the universe and everything in it in six days. He holds the Earth in His hand. He parted the red sea! But we are so arrogant that we think He cannot heal our marriage or whatever other human problem we have. We need to gain the proper perspective of our Lord. He is supernatural and in charge. He says in the Bible that even the sparrow He will nourish and how much more important to Him are we than the sparrow? He is our Father and He is just waiting to help us but we must trust Him completely in our hearts. Job 14:1-2 says:

> Man born of woman is of few days and full of trouble.
> He springs up like a flower and withers away; like a fleeting shadow, he does not endure.

We are momentary and simple. We came from dust. God is, was and always will be. His word is perfect and true. Man, a creation of His, is ridiculous in his rebellion. Imagine an ant farm for a minute. As a kid, you may have had one. Tiny ants in a plastic sleeve filled with sand working so hard and never going anywhere. They believe they are in charge of their destiny. But the truth is that if you take the ant farm and simply shake it up and down, you destroy in two seconds everything they have built and they must start over. But they work diligently in their little world and are oblivious to you, their caretaker. It is kind of amusing. But it is the same with us. We are just little ants working ourselves into a frenzy trying to control our little worlds and going nowhere. Not only is God in control of everything, but also He loves us unconditionally and with a force indescribable. That is why He sent His only son to die for our sins. He wants to be reconciled with us. I am amazed that God, creator of everything, cares for little old me. But He does and He hears my every thought. He works in my life and walks beside me every day. He speaks to my heart and leads me. Once we give up the treadmill of our lives and begin to follow the path He has laid for us, our lives can and will transform. Our hearts will be filled with love and the only two words you will ever use again to describe yourself will be peace and joy. Think about all the ways people describe themselves. I am angry or I am hurt or I am outraged or I am exhausted. I am, I am. Hamster on a wheel! Try living under God's commands for a change and trust that He is in charge. Take advice from someone who has lived both ways. A life of straying was a life of utter despair. My life now is overflowing.

WALKING IN THE DARK

WALKING IN THE DARK

The first thought I can remember clearly that formed in my mind as a result of my sin when I was twenty was about being worthless. Sin creates thoughts in your mind that are destructive. The thoughts are not true obviously but we buy into it. I am not trash! I am a child of God and I have power through Jesus to have victory in my life. All negative thoughts come from the devil. Once you realize that one simple truth, you are equipped when it happens. Then you can rebuke the devil, as the Bible instructs us to do, and he will flee and the thought with it. He will be back with a fresh lie but you will be ready to rebuke him again. Because I was not in church, not in the Word, not in prayer, I was completely unequipped for Satan's attack. I was walking alone relying on myself, which was a disaster. The Bible tells us your heart is a deceiver. People are ruled by emotion if they are not ruled by the Holy Spirit. This means they are ruled by a power they cannot trust for it is languid and misguided. I walked alone never knowing God was standing just outside my heart knocking to come in. I was in so much pain and could not see my way out. I never reached out to God. I reached out to everything else. I was drinking alcohol to numb myself from my constant negative thoughts and to feel pretty. And I was sleeping around because it made me feel desirable and powerful and temporarily loved. After the weekend, I would feel terrible physically and depressed over my sin. Sleeping around left me feeling empty after the power trip had worn off. It also made me go out looking for more. I needed to feel powerful again. I did not connect the fact that the more I slept around, the worse I felt inside and the more of my soul I gave away. Pretty soon, I did not even know how to be in a relationship. I wanted to have someone to care about me. But I either slept with him on first meeting and he wanted nothing more, or if I found a guy who wanted more, I treated him badly until it was ruined. That is because I was full of pain and confusion. I felt like I had a twenty- ton anvil strapped around my neck and I was helpless to the thoughts in my head. I was always unhappy and not only did I not know how to fix it, I didn't even know why I was unhappy. You can't really fix something if can't even understand it. So I walked around in darkness feeling hopeless and angry. I had good days and I had really bad days. The junk in my head kept me prisoner. It crippled me emotionally. It is funny to me now that I walked around so lonely feeling like no one loved me when God was standing right beside me with a love waiting that literally cannot be measured. Now that I am living in His love, I understand that no human could come anywhere close to the love He gives me. Not even the most loving wonderful person in my life can come within miles of what he gives. So it was there waiting for me the whole time! I believe that because I was baptized at nine, He would not give up on me. The thought of ending everything came and went. I told myself that I was fine, I was in control, and life was good. But deep down, I knew I was kidding myself. I knew that I was drowning. Now that I have left the wilderness and live in clarity, I can look back and realize that my life was spent feeling sorry for myself. I did not even realize that was what I was doing at the time! Imagine how many people out there live the exact same way. It is easy to do and it will make you miserable. I have said before that if the devil can get you to focus on yourself, he will defeat you. The focus on you can be good or bad. For me, it was bad but some people focus on their careers or their personal growth and this too can have the same result. Focusing on yourself rather than God completely tips the scales out of balance. In other words, there is nothing wrong with caring about your career and there is nothing wrong with wanting to better yourself intellectually. However, our first priority is supposed to be on our relationship with God understanding that the other stuff will fall into place. He will take care of our needs. It is a hard pill to swallow. I will never forget the first time I heard a preacher say that we were supposed to submit to God's will and lose our self. He said "give yourself over and count your will as nothing." I remember thinking "now wait just a minute. That is a bit much. I am in control. I am not ready to stop having fun yet. I can handle this and I want God in my life but in moderation!" I can remember how strongly I felt and how uncomfortable the thought of submission was to me. Now that I have completely submitted to God's will, I find it ridiculous that I ever thought I should be in charge! Every person has a weakness to a certain sin. For some it is gambling, some it is infidelity, some it is the love of money and success. For me it was alcohol. I carried around the pain of my parent's divorce close to me. I did not know how to heal from it. Also, my only desire that I could focus on was finding someone to love me. Through that insecurity the devil used alcohol to bring me down. I abused alcohol for several years. I became someone I didn't even recognize. And this led to me becoming someone who trusted no one. After my parents divorced, I became angry with all men. I no longer trusted them at all. I was angry, resentful, and uncaring. I remember when the Oklahoma City bombing happened and I felt nothing. I had become so numb with apathy; I had no compassion left in my heart. I felt sorry for myself, oh yes, but I had stopped caring about anyone else. Feeling sorry for myself was the way the devil steered me away from my path of victory. And the devil was right there with me convincing me to believe my darkest thoughts. I believed I was alone. I believed God was so far away. I believed no one cared about me. I wanted to just give up." The devil will urge us forward in our backward thinking. We need to realize that feeling sorry for ourselves is a waste of time, pure and simple. We need to grow up and start sowing seeds of righteousness in our own lives. If you spend your time loving people instead of yourself, God will bring healing to your own heart. And keep in mind that while we are lost in a dark hole of self- pity, the devil himself is petitioning God on our behalf that we are sinners. He is a manipulator and a liar. He will help you think backwards because he is planning your destruction. Try to remember that anytime you entertain negative thinking or indulge in sinful living, you are holding hands with the devil. I am speaking figuratively of course. But what I mean is that all sin is of the devil whether it is our thoughts or actions. If you decide to agree with those things that are offensive in the sight of the Lord, you are in fact joining forces with the evil one. You don't think of it that way because everyone on some level believes they are a good person. The fact is that negative thinking comes from the devil and it is never harmless. We need to rebuke negative thoughts always or go to God in prayer and let Him dissolve them. Little negative thoughts are a big deal because those thoughts will saturate your soul and change your perception. When you take one simple negative thought such as 'all men are cheaters' and you nurture that thought and keep it close to your heart, your mind will slowly change toward men in a way you will not even be aware of. Before you know it, you will no longer trust any men and you will walk around disappointed all the time. This thought is not only negative but it is also irrational. All men are not untrustworthy and men are not the enemy. You have one enemy and his name is Lucifer. He will try and convince you of enemies that don't exist while telling you that he is your friend. He is the only enemy and every sin is derived from him. Keep your mind clear and your focus on God and you can see the devil coming from a mile away. But if you entertain the ugly thoughts, it will cloud your mind with a bunch of junk and it will warp your perception of the truth. Be careful! Guard your mind as you do your heart. The devil attacks both.

The second lie my conscience told me was "you are never going to get married or have children. You will always be alone." When you believe these powerful lies, it will destroy your life through your mind. I only hung around the wrong kind of people. I had no real friends outside of my one best friend. Sometimes, I would feel a tug of guilt, a twinge of shame, and I would quickly silence the feeling by getting drunk. When you live in the dark, your life will spiral out of control. My life became one long night of getting drunk, sleeping with a stranger, and trying to muster the emotional energy to get through another day. I found some refuge in writing poetry. In my poetry, I could release my anguish on paper. I remember wondering if anyone out there could see me drowning, could anyone help me. Could anyone save me? I had fallen so far away from God's grace; I couldn't even feel Him anymore. In that time, He actually never left my side. I also found refuge in my family. I have the most wonderful family but even they could not help me. Only God can save you from yourself. I remember during this time going to church once in a while but feeling cold there. I did not pray. And my guilt told me often that I had sunk too low from God's reach. I reminded me of my sin daily and told myself that any hopes of living a Christian life were out of the question. I believed that I had failed. I realize now that the desire to be loved did not result from my parent's divorce. My desire to be loved and the loneliness I felt was from my separation with God. The pain I felt came from that. But the devil had me believing all these crazy lies and that I should cling to anything that comforted me. Shame will close the door. I can remember looking in the mirror and thinking "who are you?" and being disgusted with my behavior. But the shame kept me from searching for the light of God's truth. Imagine being blind. If you suddenly lost your eyesight, you would stumble around in the dark trying to find your way. What if you were in a cave alone with no light? You would probably never find your way out because you would wander aimlessly in the dark right? What if you had a flashlight? With light, the outcome is completely different. You can navigate with light. I had no light. I was walking around blind in sin and bound in misery. Now that I am walking with God, I have the power to bind the devil instead of the other way around. I live in sunshine all the time.

SALVATION

SALVATION

When I was twenty- four, I went on a date with a guy who told me while on the date, that I was lost and going to Hell. I don't think he was trying to witness to me necessarily. I remember him saying it like it was a simple fact. He told me that my lifestyle was not Christian and if I died, I was not going to Heaven. I was so offended. I couldn't believe he could say such a thing. I thought "he doesn't even know me!" I knew that I thought of God often wishing he would rescue my heart. Even though I would not turn to God and repent, I felt like God must feel sorry for me since I felt sorry for myself. And I felt like since I had been baptized at age nine, I was definitely going to Heaven even though I had no relationship with the Lord. Once saved, always saved, right? Well, I knew that was the last date I would have with this guy, And I decided right then and there, I would not be having sex with him either. How dare he judge me?

What was his agenda? So I sent him home that night and as I lay in bed, I couldn't get past what he said. I did not get much sleep that night and for the next few days, I was very irritable. God was starting to deal with me and convict my heart and I wrestled with Him. My aunt had gotten me a Bible around the same time and I remember feeling a little angry about it. I told myself I would not be reading that. So God dealt with me over the next several weeks. You see, when you are straying and someone reveals that to you, you are going to become defensive. This is not something you will want to hear. I can remember strangers asking me if I had ever received Jesus as my personal savior and I would become so irritated and think the person was being rude and intrusive. The truth is not always easy. One night, I was overcome with sorrow and I began to pray to God as I lay in bed in the dark. I prayed that God would come into my heart and take over. I also prayed for forgiveness of my sins and mercy on my soul. I instantly felt a physical hand reaching in and grabbing hold of my heart. Even though I was lying in bed, I felt like I was being pulled upward and I envisioned my body being pulled up out of a muddy grave deep in the earth. I was overcome with emotion and then a sudden feeling of peace entered my heart. I believe I was saved that night. That was the first time I had felt God's presence in my soul since I was nine. And the feeling was so much stronger this time. I immediately started going to church, praying and reading the Bible. This time I learned more because I was older. I read the New Testament and really began to get my first glimpse into the heart of Jesus. The maturity of a Christian is a curious thing. God reveals himself to us in levels. When someone first becomes saved, they are like a new born baby. A baby does not come out of the womb eating steak. He only drinks milk sometimes for the whole first year. My son did. It is the same with our faith. God is only going to reveal Himself to us as we grow on a level that we can understand. I remember trying to read the Old Testament and quickly giving up. A Christian co-worker of mine told me at the time that it was fine that I didn't understand any of it. He became a mentor to me and I am grateful for him. The New Testament and especially the Gospel of John contains everything I needed to know. It is the milk. As we grow in our walk with God, we will reach new levels of understanding and new levels of intimacy with our Father. The problem is that as soon as a person begins their walk, Satan tries to sabotage it. He attacks the young because they are most vulnerable. I say young meaning young in their relationship with God. This baby stage is so precarious because this stage is so new. It is important that a person reach out to another Christian who is more mature in their walk, a mentor, who can guide them in the beginning. I believe God sends us people for this purpose and we have to pay attention. He sent me this coworker and I did go to him in the beginning. Unfortunately, when trouble started, I did not confide in this person. At twenty- four, I felt the Holy Spirit come to reside in my heart. I remember the peace I felt that year while I was walking with God. I was new so I did not understand that Satan was going to come after me. It is not enough just to read the Bible. It is imperative that you fill your life with teaching so that you learn how to apply it to your daily life. Whether that is through study groups or listening to tapes or whatever the mode is, it is important that you do it. Think of a soldier. He is getting ready to be sent off to war to defend his country. Imagine that he is given weapons and no training on how to use those weapons. Well, he is in trouble, right? He is going face to face with the enemy who will be firing on him directly and he has weapons and no knowledge of how to use them. Most likely, he will be shot before he figures out how to load his gun. It is the same with us. Satan is powerful and that is the first thing we need to understand. Now once we are saved, we are actually more powerful than him through the power of Christ. However, if we do not understand this, it will do us no good. We have to guard our hearts and minds with God's truth the way a soldier guards his body in battle. So I was new in Christ and very happy but I was doing nothing to equip myself from impending disaster. I did not seek out fellowship with other Christians. I just went to church and read the Bible. I was already setting myself up for failure but didn't know it. The first thing I deceived myself with was taking a vow of chastity. You cannot fix yourself. God sanctifies us and removes our sins over time as we become obedient to Him. We are supposed to turn away from our sin but in doing so, we must remember that we can only succeed with God's help. We must pray for God to change us. I should have realized that if I could follow a vow of chastity on my own, what would I need God for? As soon as soon as I faltered, the devil was right there using my guilt to convince me of the next lie: "you can't be good enough to be a Christian. You are a sinner. Stop trying to be something you are not and just live a moderately Christian life. God is okay with that and I will leave you alone." Once you have received the gift of salvation, it is imperative that you educate yourself with God's Word. You must equip yourself with the truths of God so that you will live a victorious life walking with God. If you do not do that, you will fall away while the devil convinces you of so many lies. We must guard our hearts and minds with the Word of God. I was very disappointed in myself and I remember thinking that I could never succeed at being chaste. I never prayed about it because I believed God was disappointed in me too. I never realized that I could just ask for forgiveness and start again. The Bible tells us his mercy is new every morning. Now, when I fall into sin, I immediately go to God in prayer and ask forgiveness. Then I move on and I grow from it. I do not beat myself up about it. I will never be perfect. Psalm 119:75-77 teaches us that God will convict us of our sin out of love. Just like a parent will discipline their child, God will do the same for us. The verse says:

> *I know, O Lord that your laws are righteous, and in faithfulness you have afflicted me. May your unfailing love be my comfort, according to your promise to your servant. Let your compassion come to me that I may live, for your law is my delight.*

When I falter in sin, I realize that the devil is right there trying to convince me to "give up on this "and now I see it for what it is. This makes me stronger and I can avoid that sin later. I now see the devil coming more than I used to. When I am about to engage in sin of any kind, I now usually recognize it and can stand back and actually contemplate it. This is God's gift of discernment. Then I usually am able to realize what is happening. The devil has set his trap and is trying to bait me. God will reveal this to me and I can pray and simply walk in the other direction. Walking away from sin was really hard at first but has become easier and easier the more I do it. As God changes my heart, walking away from sin becomes something that gives me joy. It is hard in the beginning because as God is changing your heart, it feels kind of foreign. That is because it is. It is righteousness which your soul is not used to. Let's face it. Your soul is accustomed to sin and things of the flesh. So of course, this new skin feels funny at first. That is why so many people end up riding the fence of morality their whole lives. They cannot give themselves over completely. They do not trust in God's sanctification. The thing about sin that God wants us to understand is that as humans, we will never be perfect. However, we have been freed from the power of sin through the blood of Jesus. He wants us to pick up this weapon and learn how to use it. He wants us to be strong and confident expects us to fight the enemy and in doing so realize we are on the winning team! We were not meant to go through this life defeated and sad. We were meant to go through this life with victory and joy! It does not mean that becoming a Christian ensures a life without pain or tragedy. But it does seal your eternity and bring a peace that is so deeply rooted in your soul that life's journey is clear in the midst of loss and pain. Take a long look at your life. Are you happy deep down inside or are you ever searching to fill the void? Turn your life over to God and your life will become something you will think is too good to be true. Can you imagine that? I have it. If I have it, anyone can. Trust me. I made a life out of being miserable. I am an expert. God's presence in my life is a freedom that is so beautiful that I would trade everything in my life for it.

As I was saying, I fell away from God and it amazes me how quickly I went back into darkness. How sad to start a relationship so precious and walk away from it after only a year and lose it. The whole reason people stray in my opinion is that they don't understand that God loves us and will forgive us. I need you to understand that when I say that God loves us, I mean He loves every person He has ever created and He loves us all the same. He loves me as much as He loves His saints. That might be hard to swallow for most of us because deep down we all hold onto the notion that our deeds are what saves us. I am here to tell you that He loves us all the same. God took Saul, a murderer, and used him for His glory. Saul, who was probably the most evil man in the New Testament, was transformed into the Apostle Paul. We all know him as the man whom after his transformation lived and breathed solely to please God and spread the Gospel. It should warm your heart to know that even though you may feel a million miles from God's heart, He knows every hair on your head. He is your Father. You have complete access to Him through prayer. As I was saying, people don't understand that God loves us and will forgive us when we ask. As soon as we realize that we still have the urge for sin, we become so disenchanted that we give up. Being saved is a transformation of the heart and a renewing of the mind. However, as humans we are a work in progress. Once I finally got this and stopped telling myself I was unworthy, I was able to allow God to work on changing my heart, thus changing my behavior and eventually changing me into a new person. We hinder God with our self- doubt and guilt. The negative thoughts allow Satan to get a foothold. I was saved but carrying around guilt for being a sinner. Jesus died so we could live our lives without guilt! Because He took on our sin and died as our substitute, we stand in front of God clothed in righteousness. This righteousness is a gift from Jesus. In carrying around guilt after salvation, it is much like saying "Thank you Jesus for what you did, but if you don't mind, I am just going to continue to hang my head." We cannot earn our own worthiness! The first lesson on sin comes from Genesis 3 which covers the fall of man. It is the chapter that explains how Eve was deceived by the serpent to eat from the tree that God had commanded both Adam and Eve to stay away from or they would surely die. Adam ate from the tree also and mankind was doomed from that moment. Man was forever separated from God at this point. My point is that man is born into sin. You have no chance of walking through this life without sin even after you are saved. The world needed a savior early in our history for this reason. The second lesson is that no matter how "good" we are those good deeds amount to nothing in the sight of our Lord. He is holy. We cannot even conceive of how holy he really is. Isaiah 64:6 says:

> *All of us have become like one who is unclean, and all our righteous acts are like filthy rags; we all shrivel up like a leaf, and like the wind our sins sweep us away.*

You have to realize that nothing you ever do will save you. Nothing you ever do will deem you worthy to stand in God's presence. You are a sinner who deserves to go to Hell. Salvation is a gift to us that we receive by His grace through our faith. That is all. We are supposed to spend our lives after salvation in search of the heart of Jesus. However, in that search, we are to remember that we will never attain worthiness through anything we ever do. For years I have heard preachers say this in church and it never sunk in with me. So it is no surprise that as soon as I messed up, I gave up and I slowly got into partying again but hey, not as much. And I started sleeping around again but not as much and not without shame. When you walk away from God, you do not fall into a valley, you plunge over the cliff.

WALKING IN THE WILDERNESS

WALKING IN THE WILDERNESS

I was baptized for the second time in my life in March of 1995 and in just two years went back to my old lifestyle. What a shame. I went to church once in a while but that did not last. Soon after I fell away, I met my first husband. I won't say much concerning this except that I married a man who was not a Christian and entered into a miserable existence. I was distracted the first two years of this marriage with my grandmother's battle with lung cancer and eventual passing. All my free time was spent with her and I ignored what was going on in my own house. Her death is the hardest thing I have ever gone through and I didn't think I could go on without her. Of course, I had no choice. After she passed, my focus was fully back on the marriage and soon I was abusing alcohol and pain killers on a daily basis to cope. My husband was verbally abusive among other things and I started entertaining suicide again. But this time the voice was clearer and stronger. My grandmother came to me in a dream and told me to snap out of it. So I did. That visit from her was so real to me that I actually did snap out of my pity party. I put the alcohol and the drugs down and got myself physically and mentally healthy again. I started going to church again and eventually escaped my marriage. The escape happened when God used the one person I have always admired to speak up frankly about my husband. It was my granddaddy. My granddaddy is the kind of man I call hero. He worked all of his adult life in a mill to provide for his wife and three children. He still works at the ripe old age of eighty at a part time job. He was in earlier years a volunteer fireman and that in and of itself is commendable. But when you find out he has only one arm, then he really gets your attention. He also drove an ambulance for a while. I never noticed that arm growing up in a way that people notice handicaps. It was all I knew, not to mention that he has never acted handicapped. He does everything a man with two arms can do, including carpentry and working on cars. The only thing he cannot do is tie his shoes. So he wears Velcro. Besides the adversity he has overcome in his life physically after losing his arm in an accident in the mill, he also overcame an abusive father. My granddaddy takes after his mother meaning that he is full of love. He is gentle and kind. We are close like father and daughter. I am so lucky to have him. He has done so much for me. He is the one who always changed the oil in my car when it needed it, picked me up at school when it snowed, took me to see "Bo Duke" from the Dukes of Hazard at the coliseum on my tenth birthday because it was my favorite show and showed me physical affection when I was sick.

Actually, he is physically affectionate all the time. He loves hugs and kisses. My granddaddy and I have never hidden anything from each other. We always shoot straight with each other and tell each other what we are thinking. And I mean about the big things in life. How many people can say they have that kind of relationship with their grandfather? I can remember being little and sitting on the couch with granddaddy watching The Lawrence Welk show and thinking there was no other place in the world I would rather be. I can remember him walking home from the mill for lunch when was I little. We lived down the hill. Back then, they built neighborhoods around the mill. Everyone who worked in the mill lived in that neighborhood and so it was walking distance. He would come down the hill whistling because he is always whistling. He would have those earplugs they wore in the mill draped around his neck and when he saw me he would smile and say "well hello pumpkin". His smile lit up my world and still does. My grandparents have loved me in a way that I could never repay. I know in my heart I am blessed beyond measure. I realize now that my granddaddy must have had such a hard time holding his tongue the first time I was married. And I believe after my grandmother died, he finally reached a point where he decided to follow his heart and tell me what he thought. I will never forget it. I was sitting in the kitchen and my granddaddy walked in and he said simply " I just want to say one thing and I will shut up. Your grandmother would never have put up with me treating her the way your husband treats you." That was all I needed to hear. There was no judgment in his voice and no disappointment, only sadness. I nodded my head silently and we have never spoken of it again to this day. But I left that marriage right after that and started over.

It did not take long for me in my new single status to start riding the fence of Christian slash moderate sinner. I know now what I did not know then. Once you are walking with God, you must keep in mind that you are human and subject to temptation. Therefore, you must arm yourself with God's arsenal if you plan on walking with the flock and not straying. The devil will come at you in a very subtle ways when you first start walking with God. He knows it is the little things that can and will chip away at your victory. He knows all he has to do is slip in with some discouragement. For example, maybe your friends you used to party with no longer understand you. Maybe they even make fun of you, or stop being your friends altogether. Things like this can be so hurtful especially if they come from someone we care about. Now if you are not prepared for Satan's attack, it could be enough to get you to pull back away from God. As soon as you do that, you are doomed. If you are prepared, you will take it to God in prayer where he will comfort you. He will also send folks to you who will confirm what he tells you. God uses people for these purposes and it will be totally unbeknownst to them. Also, God will direct you through scripture. Matthew 5:11-12 says:

> *Blessed are you when people insult you, persecute you and falsely say all kinds of evil against you because of me. Rejoice and be glad, because great is your reward in heaven, for in the same way they persecuted the prophets who were before you.*

So it is one thing to receive salvation. It is quite another to remain in God's grace and grow as a Christian. The "how to for dummies" is in Ephesians. Unfortunately for me, I did not find this most important information until later on. Ephesians 6:10-18 is to me one of the most important passages in the Bible and it reads:

> Finally, be strong in the Lord and in his mighty power. Put on the full armor of God so that you can take your stand against the devil's schemes. For our struggle is not against flesh and blood, but against the rulers, against the authorities, against the powers of this dark world and against the spiritual forces of evil in the heavenly realms. Therefore, put on the full armor of God, so that when the day of evil comes, you may be able to stand your ground, and after you have done everything, to stand. Stand firm then, with the belt of truth buckled around your waist, with the breastplate of righteousness in place, and with your feet fitted with the readiness that comes from the gospel of peace. In addition to all this, take up the shield of faith, with which you can extinguish all the flaming arrows of the evil one. Take the helmet of salvation and the sword of the Spirit, which is the word of God. And pray in the Spirit on all occasions with all kinds of prayers and requests. With this in mind, be alert and always keep praying for all the saints.

How wonderful this passage is. It explains how to safeguard your heart from Satan! My favorite is the part about the shield of faith extinguishing the arrows of Satan. Faith is the cornerstone of Christianity. We readily refer to being a Christian as "our faith" but how many of us actually walk in faith? That was always my problem. I did not trust the Lord to run my life. I would say that I had turned to God and then I would continue to walk in my will and not His. That means that I did not have faith that He knew better for me than I knew for myself! And when you try to run your own life and don't submit everything to God, the devil is waiting around the corner. It amazes me when a Christian tells me they are miserable in some area in their life. I will ask them if they took it to God in prayer and left it with Him. They always answer with a languid "well, I prayed about it over and over but..." and I will say "but you didn't leave it With Him did you?" and their response will be "well, not really. I just keep trying to fix it myself" I then say "how is that working out for you? Oh yes, you are miserable!" The creator of the universe who made you and knew all your days before time began can handle any problem in your little life you throw at Him. Try it. That is all He is waiting for. Once you give him your problem in faith, He will handle it. In his perfect timing and omnipotence, He will work in your life. Too many Christians don't even believe that God is capable of working in their lives. So what is the point? Think of it like this. For those of you who have children, do you believe your toddler knows better than you do what is good for him or her? Ridiculous right? It is the same thing with God. Do you have your toddler's best interest at heart? Would you give your child anything and everything within your power? Would you do anything in your means to protect your child from harm or being sad? Do you feel that if your child will listen to you, you can help him or her avoid a lot of mistakes? It is the same with God. We are His children, literally, and He feels the same way. But we are far more stubborn than the most unruly child. Pride and arrogance is man's folly. The Bible actually addresses this in Matthew 18:3-4:

> *And he said: I tell you the truth, unless you change and become like little children, you will never enter the kingdom of heaven. Therefore, whoever humbles himself like this child is the greatest in the kingdom of heaven.*

A NEW LIFE, SAME OLD ME

A NEW LIFE, SAME OLD ME

In 2002, I met the last man I will ever love, who is now my husband. I can say that he is the best thing that has ever happened to me. Neither one of us was walking with God when I met him but I could tell by his gentle spirit early on that he had been saved at some point. Having said that, we had fun together! We partied very hard. It was like we fueled each other's sinful desires. We also had so much in common and were so much in love that I was constantly celebrating. Well, I had found the man who would rescue me from myself! He did not know the enormous job I had given to him. I expected him to fix me. I was sure he could. We bought a house and moved in together in 2004. Very soon afterwards, I discovered I was not happy. I felt shame and guilt over our living situation and could not seem to shake the suicide thing. I began to fantasize how I would do it. The thing was, my husband is a good man and treats me well. He does not borrow trouble and like my granddaddy he is kind and gentle. But love cannot save you. A person cannot save you. Only a personal relationship with God can save you. So before long, I was back to being miserable again. And I was just as miserable as I had ever been in my life. I soon realized that my first husband had not been the source of my misery. He had only been a symptom of it. I tormented him on a daily basis. I am so thankful that he did not give up on me. I constantly threatened to leave him. I started fights with him all the time over nothing. I sat around feeling sorry for myself and crying often. I always felt disappointed in him. He probably thought I was crazy! I know for a fact that he is happy I am walking with God again. I think maybe he benefits from it more than anyone else! The devil had convinced me to live in fear and mistrust believing that one day eventually my husband would leave me. The most painful lie I ever bought into was "Your dad left your mom after twenty- one years. Of course your husband will leave you. He does not love you." God has since pointed out that not only does my husband love me but that I am his number one! I have tried to repair the damage I did to our relationship through prayer and by treating my husband the way he deserves to be treated. One thing to remember about my story is that he has not changed. He is the same man that he ever was. He still hoards empty boxes and watches sports on T.V. too much. What has changed is my heart. I try to explain to people that your partner is never the reason you are happy or unhappy. If you are unhappy in your life on any level, it is because your heart is not right with God. When you are right, you are happy no matter what your circumstances in life are. Christians have marched to their deaths singing hymns to God all the way because they were right. Just as I said before that a person can have it all and be miserable, it is the same in reverse. So you can have everything and be unhappy and you can also have nothing and be happy. Why do you think it is called being lost and being saved? It defines the core of a person. When you are lost, you are aimless and suffering. When you are saved, you are secure and full of hope.

One Sunday morning, while my now husband and I were still living together in sin, I was flipping through channels on the television and saw a man who was preaching on a live broadcast in the town we were living in. I hesitated on the channel and the preacher said "if you are having premarital sex, it is a sin. Now don't get mad at me, I didn't say it. God said it, take it up with Him." I thought to myself 'I am going to check that church out!' Even though I immediately felt guilty, I also liked the honesty and the blunt way he put that. Pretty soon, I was going to that church. And I felt something there I had never really felt before at other churches I had visited. I now know it is the Holy Spirit I am referring to. At the time, I just knew it was something powerful. This was in 2005 and I was thirty -four years old. I went for about a year before I strayed this time. This time I stopped going because someone in the church hurt my feelings. Wow! How pathetic has my faith been?

Let's do a quick recap of my straying. I strayed in my teens, I strayed at twenty- six, I strayed at thirty- two, and then again at thirty-four. I have strayed more than I have walked and I have spent more time outside God's grace than in it. I have always felt His presence my whole life even when I wasn't living for Him. Once you are saved, His presence is always there even though we try to ignore it. Well, my husband and I were married in 2006 and I had my son in 2007. My child is definitely the greatest joy in my life. I never knew I could love someone that much! What an incredible experience and what an incredible bond! I have never known anything like it. Now, do you want to hear the scariest part of this story? I have contemplated suicide since I became a mother. I am ashamed to admit this of course but if I am going to speak the truth of God, I must speak the truth of me. Why would I ever think about that again? Well, I had strayed again right before I got married and so I was vulnerable. However, for the first time in my life, that contemplation filled me with fear. I knew that my son needed a mother and I felt really guilty that I had those thoughts again but remember that at this time, I still had not connected these thoughts to my straying. I still did not understand. It was when I came back to my final walk as I call it in the spring of 2008 that finally everything became clear to me. I was thirty-seven and I call it my final walk because for the first time in my life, I really got it. For the first time, I dove into the Bible and honestly studied it. For the first time, I went to God in earnest prayer. And for the first time, I committed myself to the church. As a result, God revealed Himself to me in a way that I will never turn my back on Him again. God knows your heart and reveals Himself to us as we commit it to Him. I do not expect to be perfect but the difference this time is that I have completely surrendered my life to His will. I believe the circumstances surrounding my final eye-opening deliverance back to the flock involved my workplace. Sometimes, when we stray too long, He will allow things to go very wrong in our lives to get our attention. I think God had truly become fed up with me. I do not wish to be too specific regarding the circumstances but I do want to describe how unhappy I became. Imagine going to a job every day and you are so miserable there that you feel physically ill when you pull into the parking lot. Maybe you don't need to imagine it because it is currently your situation. If so, you need to listen extra hard! Due to a situation with an employee that had been hired by my company, my life at work went from a content existence to something so miserable that it totally consumed me. Had I not had a mortgage and a child, I would have walked out. But I did have a mortgage and a child so I was forced to swallow my very dignity and show up every day. I have never been so angry and felt so hopeless in my life. I worked so hard to get where I was and I had been with the company for a long time. At first, because I was so humiliated and treated so unfairly, I started looking for another job. I spent hours writing up resumes and emailing them every night. I also spent every night in tears. I never got a single interview after months of trying. I finally realized I was not meant to leave the company so I started thinking about what it all meant. Then I started to pray about it and God was right there to comfort me. He revealed to me that He would change my situation if I would stop trying and put all my energy and focus on our relationship. So I did. For the next year or so, I worked hard and kept my head down. I ignored everything that was going on around me and took it to God in prayer every night. I read aloud from the book of Psalm every night as well because it has always had a way of comforting me when I am down. You can find verses in there that will apply to exactly what you are going through. No matter what it might be! So I found the verses concerning this situation and I read it every single night. I went back to the church I had left in 2006 and rekindled my love for it. In that time period, God let me suffer for a while and I suddenly understood that I was going through this for a reason. God reassured me that He was in control of the whole thing and that I did not need to understand it all. It was also necessary for me to get that I needed God in my life and that I was lost without Him. I finally got it! I stopped caring about my career and where it was headed and just focused on working hard every day. My total mission became centered on reconciliation with and instruction from God. God eventually dealt with the situation and I was restored to my prior position, regained respect and my salary increased beyond what I could have imagined! I look back on that time and even though it was the hardest thing I have ever gone through in my life, outside of losing my grandmother, I know that this was the best thing that could have happened to me. If not for this, I would not be walking with God right now. Even though the devil was attacking me through this situation, God used even the bad to ultimately fulfill his good end. I have since forgiven anyone who was involved and now I appreciate my job so much more. I work harder and I treat those I come in contact with on a daily basis with compassion and encouragement. I actually found a love for my career that wasn't there before and so I am grateful.

I WAS LOST, NOW I AM FOUND

I WAS LOST, NOW I AM FOUND

My life is very different now these past three years. I love my husband and son dearly and I enjoy the life we have together. I enjoy my job and I use it as a door to witness to people every single day. I no longer care about the material things. Most of the time, I am no longer needy or full of anxiety. I experience the wonder of each new day. God has blessed me with family and good health. I now have four women that I call best friends who care about me and are always there for me. I cherish their friendship. I am a member of the church that I love. I could go on and on naming out my blessings but I think you get the picture. The Bible tells us that if you are obedient to His word, He will fulfill the desires of your heart. He has done that for me and beyond. There is nothing else that matters now except my walk and my continued growth in the Lord. I am blessed beyond measure and my cup overflows. Do you want this for yourself? Do you believe after what I have told you that you can have it? Belief in the unseen is the only thing you need to grasp to attain what I have. You think you know what you need to be happy but you don't. I promise that you don't have a clue. But he does. He knows exactly what you need because he created you. He formed your heart. Sometimes I am so happy, I feel like I am outside of my world looking in. I cannot even believe it. And the things that make me so happy are nothing that I ever thought would fill me with such gladness. It scares me to think about where I would be if He had just given me everything I thought I needed. Once I gave in and left everything up to Him, He immediately fixed it all. Have you ever tried opening a jar of something and the lid is on so tight that you cannot budge it? So of course you try and try to turn it to the point you usually hurt your hand. Why? Because you are stubborn! Eventually, after you are completely frustrated, you hand the jar to someone else and they turn it with complete ease and it opens! It is the same with God. Our heart is the lid and He can turn it with ease because He is the keeper of it. We cannot even budge it because we are clueless to its mechanics. It is a complete mystery to us. We try to open the jar because by nature we are stubborn, prideful, and full of sin. These factors deceive us into believing we are smarter than God. As my grandmother used to say "we get too big for our breeches!" We spend our lives trying to open the jar and the only result is frustration and pain. People are usually afraid to say straight up that they think they are smarter than God. But the fact is that if you try to run the show that is exactly what you are saying to Him. One of these days you will get tired of trying to open the jar. You will stop and realize you are exhausted. When this happens, contemplate who made the jar. The one who crafted it loves you and cares about every facet of you. He is in control of the universe and would love nothing more than to open the jar for you. Talk to Him and see Him respond to you. It will amaze you how personal our savior is with those who seek Him. Turn to God and He will do the rest.

I recently had someone very close to me say that God did not involve Himself in our daily lives. This person believes in God but he doesn't believe that we can get that close to the creator. He believes that God runs things from afar, a loving but distant God who takes care of major matters but doesn't have time for the little things. That is one of the saddest things I have ever heard anyone say. If you believe that God doesn't have time for each person, you have missed the whole show. My entire point is that God is a personal God. He used to walk with Adam and Eve in the Garden of Eden every day! Think about all the people of the Bible that God either directly spoke to or gave revelation of Himself through a miracle or a vision. God reveals Himself to those who trust in Him. And I believe He reveals Himself more and more as our relationship with Him deepens. What would be the point of seeking a deep personal relationship with God if He kept us at a distance? I know a preacher who says that God spoke to him one night as he slept on a submarine when he was in the navy. He audibly heard God's voice. I am here to tell you that God speaks to me all the time. It has never been audible. But His voice speaks to me in a way that I know it is not coming from my own thoughts. His voice is very discernible to me. God moves in my life in a way that can only be explained by the fact that God is right beside me. Why would Jesus die for us if He didn't have time for a relationship with us? We are His children. Think about the bond you have with your child. Let's say the child wanted nothing to do with you. Think about the pain this would cause you. God longs for reconciliation with us. He loves us so much more than we can comprehend. The way you love your kids is only a taste of the way God loves us. I think once you really realize how personal God is, you will start to crave a relationship with Him too.

Everything in the world without Jesus is all for naught. Everyone outside of God's grace is like the gazelle I was talking about earlier. Give her food, children, sun, shelter, and a beautiful landscape. The tiger will still come and kill her. And there is nothing she can do to stop him. She cannot fight him. She is ill quipped. Imagine a gazelle trying to fight a tiger. That is a sad picture to envision because we know gazelles are by nature helpless. It is the same way with humans and the devil. Without God, he will come and destroy your life. It is only a matter of when. Think about a celebrity you know that has died in a lonely hotel room of a drug overdose. There are plenty to choose from. They had fortune, fame, access to anything their hearts could ever desire and they are dead. How sad is that? All of that stuff means nothing.

When someone comes to me and tells me how miserable they are and they are not walking with the Lord, I just literally want to scream at them and say "the answer is so simple!" Your life is a mess, you have ruined your marriage, your finances are in the ditch, your health has started to suffer, you are angry most of the time, and you are so deep in self-pity, you cannot even see the light. Life does not have to be this way. In fact, not only does it not have to be awful, it should be full of victory. I tried to run my own life for thirty-six years and for thirty-six years I shuffled through life. Most of the time I was unhappy, didn't feel good, didn't get much accomplished, didn't really have any goals, lived in fear and anxiety and was usually disappointed in my husband and friends. When I was not walking with God, the constant lies about who I was, what I was here for and who did or didn't love me was overwhelming. I told myself that I was mediocre. All lies. Boy, when I look back over my life, I could smack myself in the forehead like the V8 commercials. Had I surrendered my life to God earlier, there is no telling what He would have done with me! He had a plan for me to bring Him glory and overflow my cup before the foundation of the world! That is amazing! I am the one who got in the way and prevented His blessings for me by leading my own sinful life. I try not to live in regret because the devil would love that too. I realize my mistakes and part of the reason I am writing this is so that others might not go as long as I did before they figure it out. I also hope my son will read this early on and get it too. But I do have victory now. God is working through me now. He still has a plan for my life, yes, even at the age of almost forty! He can do mighty things with me if I get out of the way and submit to His will. I cannot conceive of all that He can do for and through me. My doubt will prevent but my faith will powerfully allow His miracles in my life. Now I feel God urging me forward to write my testimony so I am. Once you surrender control, it is actually very exciting to sit back and watch what He does with your life. You don't know what is around the corner but you know it is good.

Think about someone you know who is living outside God's grace or straying. They are trying to lead their own life and failing miserably at it. People who stray lose sight of the truth. It is like losing your compass on a hike. As a result, they completely lose sight of right and wrong and fall into what feels good for them instead. Proverbs 4:19 says:

> But the way of the wicked is like deep darkness; they do not know what makes them stumble.

This means that when people lose sight of God, they lose their way literally and come under control of the devil. They are unaware of the sin they are slipping into and the destruction it holds for their future. For example, I know people who become obsessed with playing the lottery and get rich quick schemes. I want to ask them what they think being rich will accomplish. Okay, so maybe you could buy a bigger house or travel. But think about the new problems that would surface. People would come out of the woodwork with their hands held out. You would have to figure out who you would and would not help. It would be very stressful. You would be trying to protect your money all the time. I have watched a documentary on the outcome of lottery winners. The show had one couple who ended up okay. Most ended up divorced or losing all the money in foolish investments. One committed suicide. One was murdered by his two sisters. I also know Christians who have almost no money and no real assets. They spend all their time helping others and enjoying their families and these people do not have a care in the world. They are happy and content. I believe you need to spend your time working with what God gave you. If you have to work every day for a paycheck, God expects you to go to that job with a good attitude and do your very best. What a waste to sit around all the time to fantasize about what you do not have. Who cares? Your time here is short. God promises us mansions in heaven. Matthew 25:34 says:

> *Then the King will say to those on his right, 'Come, you who are blessed by my Father; take your inheritance, the kingdom prepared for you since the creation of the world.*

Also, God addresses the wealthy here on Earth when he says in Matthew 19:24:

> *Again, I tell you, it is easier for a camel to go through the eye of a needle than for a rich man to enter the kingdom of God.*

Does this mean that if you have money that you don't have salvation? Of course not. However, He is saying that a man who is rich is most likely owned by his wealth. People are consumed by money. Spend time with someone who is wealthy. A lot of people, who are either wealthy or striving for wealth think, breathe and live money. It is on their lips all the time. Whatever consumes you will be on your lips all the time. If you are consumed with Earthly desires, there will be no room for God.

Coming back to the flock is easy. The devil will try to convince you that it is not. He will incite guilt, shame and even fear. The truth is that coming back is the most natural thing you can do but it must be done with a contrite heart. You must realize that you have nothing to bring to the table. You must be broken to this life you lead. You only need three simple words to transform your mind, body and soul. They are: turn to God.

Turn to God. It is so simple. This sentence is in the very first paragraph of this book. I turned to God.

That is all. God will stand behind you. He will walk beside you. But you must first be willing to turn to Him. That means that you must repent of your sins and turn your heart over to Him. You must realize that you cannot be in charge anymore and that you need Him. When you finally reach out to God in prayer, He will be right there to pick you up off your knees and fill you with a renewed strength and a new heart. You will feel His forgiveness wash over you. You will feel your life become your whole life ahead of you once again. The Word will then be the thing you cannot live without. A man converted walks with the heart of Jesus. He loves everyone, everyone. He will forgive every wrong anyone does to him, every wrong. A man converted will base every decision on God's will for his life and conform his mind to a holy goal. One who is truly saved will stand out in their daily lives against everyone else as different. He will not be popular for his actions. He will exude generosity, love, forgiveness, humility, gentleness, and will ever have God on his lips. He will stand firm in his faith and share the good news with others urgently and with fervor. If this sounds foreign to you, you might want to reexamine your heart. There is a huge difference between a healthy respect for Jesus and a broken heart for God. If you will bind up your courage and pour yourself out at the feet of Jesus, He will pick you up and set you on wings like eagles. If you don't feel the fire for Christ, never fear. He is only a prayer away.

AFTER THE LIGHT DAWNS

AFTER THE LIGHT DAWNS

My main purpose for writing this book is to make people understand the danger that lurks for every Christian once they are saved. What is important to understand is that as soon as you start walking with God and become obedient to His will, the devil will try anything to sabotage your relationship and your efforts. The devil's plan will go from keeping you lost to now encouraging you to stray. You need to be aware of that and get equipped. As I said before, Ephesians tells us how to equip ourselves with the sword of the spirit, the helmet of salvation, the armor of God. You will need to read your Bible daily, pray regularly and find a church. You will need to guard your heart and your mind. He will try anything and I mean anything to get a foothold. Pray for discernment. Be ready. The devil will even use family or friends to offend you- people you love. If you stray, you will become lost in your life. You will lose your grip on your relationship with God and you will start filling your life with false things. I think it is important to have hobbies and to have fun but a person has to keep focused or before they know it, they will be tempted. The devil uses the same lies to tempt us now as he did with Adam and Eve in the Garden of Eden. Nothing has changed. He will try to convince you that if you walk with God that you will miss out on all the fun. He will try to convince you that sin is not that big of a deal and that you have every right to live your life to the utmost discovering all the world has to offer. He will convince you that in this land of plenty you should fill your heart's desires and that you should educate yourself with the books of man to become cultured and wise. Just as Adam and Eve, we humans of the twenty first century are still foolish enough to indulge our curiosities at the risk of losing our souls! The temptations the devil uses are nothing new and nothing glamorous. He tempts with things such as sex, greed, vanity and for some even fame. Anything you feel tempted by is nothing that you are battling alone. I Corinthians 10:13 says:

> *No temptation has seized you except what is common to man. And God is faithful; he will not let you be tempted beyond what you can bear. But when you are tempted, he will also provide a way out so that you can stand up under it.*

I try to follow some simple basics: I put on love every day and carry it around and give it out freely to everyone I see. I spend time alone with God early in the morning before I start my day and late at night before bed. I feed on the Word like I do real food- it is my daily nourishment and just like if I skipped a real meal or two, skipping time with God leaves me weak and vulnerable. Did you know that if you don't eat a healthy regular diet, you are putting yourself at risk for sickness because your immunity system becomes compromised? It is the same way with God. I need His Word on my lips every day. I need His guidance on a daily basis to stay strong and clear headed. So I put on love and spend time with God. I try to imitate what Christ would do in every situation. And, when the devil does come after me, I go down on my knees in prayer. I don't think about it, I don't analyze it for days. I don't try to figure out how to fix it. I don't wallow in it. I take it to God and I leave it with Him.

In our present-day society, the world is so misled. The devil has his hand in T.V., radio, the media, magazines, you name it. Everywhere you look now all you see is sex, fortune and women with model perfect bodies. I am dismayed at how quickly things have become so accepted that just twenty or thirty years ago were not. The devil uses media as a world-wide vessel to encourage sinful living. People are influenced by behavior they watch on T.V. day after day. We don't really want to admit this but it is true nevertheless. Young children face the highest risk of course. If they grow up watching movies and programs where sex before marriage is completed normal, they will be influenced by that thinking like it or not. This is true for adults as well. We have come to believe that we must go with the flow in our modern society. I can remember thinking that no man would be willing to wait for marriage to begin a sexual relationship and that if I wanted a boyfriend then that was one thing I would have to bend on. Instead of sticking to what is right, we bend the right to fit our lives. Instead of trusting that God will take care of us if we follow His rules, we cling to what man says is okay. Not only are we bombarded with wrong images on morality, we are also bombarded with distractions. I believe technology is a good thing although I happen to be one of those people who could never figure out my VCR so never mind any of the very sophisticated things out there right now! Even though I believe technological advancement is good, overall I think the devil uses technology as a further distraction for people. The devil will try to fill our minds with empty time killers just to keep us from fellowship with God. I believe it is working. How many people do you know that go home from work every day and spend hours on the PlayStation? Okay, now how many people do you know that go home every day and study their Bible? The devil will give us things, fun things to distract us. Let us not forget also, the thing Satan is best at which is persuasion. He will try to gently start a persuasive argument. He is very subtle and manipulative. He will use your friends and family if he can. He will try to convince you oh so gently that this one sin is no big deal. Just a little taste is okay. God understands you are only human. If you entertain these thoughts, new ones will come behind them saying that you that you are probably tired and just need a little fun. He will try to wear you down without you even realizing it. Then he will speak through someone you love if he can find someone weak. Before you know it, you are saying to yourself that it really isn't that big of a deal. You just need a little break. You better watch out. Pray that God will speak to you when you become weak. Pray that He will reveal that to you and remind you of the truth. Once you are saved, you are set apart from the power of sin. This not only means it no longer holds power over you. It also means that to continue in it after your conversion will be an act of knowledge and premeditation. The Bible says God will deal with those who make Him out to be a liar. Do not lie to others. Do not lie to yourself. Most of all, do not try to deceive God. You are only deceiving yourself and when you do that, the devil has you right where he wants you. Seek God and He will find you.

FORMER ME, FOREVER GONE

FORMER ME, FOREVER GONE

Scar tissue is where something has healed over but left a mark. I have a lot of scar tissue. Most of this scar tissue is from self-inflicted wounds. These wounds might have been fatal had God not intervened. He healed me and I all I have left is scar tissue. I will wear it proudly as a symbol of survival. I am now walking with God every day and He has led me back to the flock. I will never stray again. I finally have enough truth inside me to protect myself from getting lost. I now understand the meaning of life. People spend their whole lives trying to answer this question. It says plainly in the Bible that the meaning of life is to love God and keep His commandments. I will never achieve holy. However, I understand now that only God is holy and perfect. My salvation is from His sacrifice alone and through nothing I have done. My walk is achieved through His grace and finding my way back to the flock is a gift of His mercy and love. His patience with me is something I will never understand but will always remain grateful for. I will always seek the heart of Jesus now and bask in the peace I have. If you are one of His sheep and you have strayed, I am here to tell you that it is not too late. I am here to tell you the pain and confusion in your heart is a result of your separation from your Father. And I am here to tell you that everything wrong in your life can be healed. He is waiting. Peace is a prayer away.

God has intention with your life. He wants you to live happy, fruitful and blessed. He longs for a personal relationship with you. You are born with free will meaning that God will not force His way in. It is a choice to follow Him. Personally, there is no other choice for me. I spent a lot of years doing it without Him and wandering around in circles in the wilderness. Now I walk in the sure and steady path of His footsteps surrounded by light. There is one thing I need to add to my message. The Bible tells us that God protects His sheep. What does this mean? Well, it means that if you are walking in God's grace, He will protect you during the storm. Psalm 103:6 says:

> *The Lord works righteousness and justice for all the oppressed.*

God will subdue your enemies quickly if you are obedient to Him. Psalm 103:13 says:

> *As a father has compassion on his children, so the Lord has compassion on those who fear him.*

This means He will fight your battles for you in your daily life. Think about your daily struggles and the things that happen to you that do not seem to be fair. If you are walking with God, He will bring you through your trials to His good end and your benefit. He promises to comfort you, meet all your needs, and give you a victorious life.

THE BEGINNING, THE MIDDLE, AND THE END

THE BEGINNING, THE MIDDLE AND THE END

My entire life God has used the number 23 to place significance on certain events. The grandmother I loved so dearly was born on the 23rd. I recited Psalm 23 to her in the dark as she spent her last few hours here on Earth. I met my husband on the third day of August, 2002 and we were married on June 3, 2006. Our son was born in the 3rd month and on the 2nd day. He was a day early and I have always been bothered by that but I just realized he was born exactly when God intended. When I first started writing this book, the Lord urged me to read a religious book that had been sitting on my shelf for quite some time. So I took it to work and read it that day during my breaks. The number 23 was in the title and as I was reading it, I got the strangest feeling that this book was significant. I looked over at the clock as this very thought was forming in my mind and saw that the date was the 23rd. The rest of that day the number 23 kept popping up. I told a friend I wish I knew what was so special about the number 23. This was a Wednesday so that night at church the preacher spoke a sermon on how the things of God are sometimes mysterious and that we will not always understand. Also, that night he put a formula on the big screen which was part of the sermon and the formula was full of 2's and 3's. This has been swirling around in my mind ever since waiting I guess for some meaning. Today I received it. As I was drinking in the beauty of the day and breathing in the fresh spring air, it came to me. And in the rnoment I got it, I glanced at the computer and realized that today is the 3rd! There are many other instances of the number 23 in my life but I think you get the picture. I did not realize that this number which keeps surfacing in my life meant something. I only realized it when I was finishing this book. The culmination of this entire writing resides in the number 23. It is Psalm 23 and everything in my life thus far comes down to this single passage. It explains everything I have been telling you. This has always been my favorite passage in the Bible and I carry it in my heart as I walk through this journey called life. Oh and what a beautiful journey it is! I am sitting on my patio as I write this, looking around at the gorgeous colors of spring. The birds are singing and the fragrant breeze of new flowers inspires me! Just so you know, I haven't contemplated suicide in three years and I know I never will again. The only thing I contemplate these days is the present. Today is a gift and I love each moment. My future is exciting to think about and for the first time in my life I feel like I am at my beginning! I will walk the rest of my life reciting Psalm 23 and seeking the heart of Jesus. So here we are at the end and I will finish with His words, not mine. These words sum up His magnificent and unfailing love for us. Psalm 23:

> *The Lord is my shepherd; I shall not be in want. He makes me lie down in green pastures, He leads me beside quiet waters, He restores my soul. He guides me in paths of righteousness for his name's sake. Even though I walk through the valley of the shadow of death, I will fear no evil, for you are with me; your rod and your staff, they comfort me. You prepare a table before me in the presence of my enemies. You anoint my head with oil; my cup overflows. Surely goodness and love will follow me all the days of my life, and I will dwell in the house of the Lord forever.*

CPSIA information can be obtained
at www.ICGtesting.com
Printed in the USA
FFHW021406251019
55767920-61633FF